THE WINNING MINDSET

THE ESSENTIAL GUIDE TO MENTAL STRENGTH AND RESILIENCE FOR ALL.

DR. RAJNISH KUMAWAT

Contents

PREFACE

The Winning Mindset is a guide to unlocking your full potential and achieving success in any area of your life. The book is designed to help you develop the mental and emotional tools you need to overcome obstacles and reach your goals.

Throughout the book, you will learn about the power of positive thinking, self-confidence, and visualization. You will discover how to manage stress, build resilience, and create a support system to help you achieve your goals. You will also learn about the importance of a growth mindset and how to embrace change and take calculated risks.

The Winning Mindset is not just a book about achieving success, but also about living a fulfilling life. It provides practical strategies for self-care and achieving balance in your personal and professional life. The book is filled with inspiring stories of individuals who have overcome challenges and achieved success through the power of a winning mindset.

Whether you're an entrepreneur, an athlete, a student, or simply someone looking to improve your life, The Winning Mindset is a valuable resource that will help you unlock your full potential and reach your goals.

We believe that the principles outlined in this book are the key to unlocking your full potential and achieving success. With the right mindset and the right tools, you can achieve anything you set your mind to. We hope that this book will serve as a guide and inspiration as you work towards creating the life you want.

Acknowledgements

I would like to express my sincere gratitude to the following individuals who have helped make this book, **"The Winning Mindset"**, a reality:

- My family and friends, who have provided their unwavering support and encouragement throughout this journey.
- My editor, who has provided invaluable feedback and guidance in shaping the final product.
- The countless successful individuals who have shared their insights and experiences with me, and inspired me to write this book.
- The readers who have supported me with their positive feedback and reviews.
- Finally, to all the individuals who are on a journey to develop a winning mindset, I hope this book will serve as a valuable resource and a catalyst for achieving their goals.

Thank you!

I

Introduction: The Importance of a Winning Mindset

The key to achieving success in any area of life is having a winning mindset. A winning mindset is the collection of attitudes, beliefs and habits that enable you to approach life with a positive and proactive attitude. It empowers you to achieve your goals and live a fulfilling life.

> "A winning mindset isn't just about winning, it's about striving for excellence in everything you do."

The power of a winning mindset cannot be overstated. It gives you the ability to think positively, set and achieve your goals, overcome obstacles and bounce back from setbacks. It gives you the mental toughness to push through difficult times and the resilience to overcome adversity. It enables you to maintain focus and stay motivated, even when the going gets tough.

A winning mindset is essential for anyone who wants to achieve greatness in their life. It is the foundation upon which success is built. Without it, you will struggle to achieve your goals and find fulfillment in life. With it, you will be able to overcome any challenge that comes your way and reach your full potential.

One real-life example of understanding the power of positive thinking is the story of **J.K. Rowling**, the author of the Harry Potter series. Despite facing rejection from multiple publishers, she never gave up on her dream of becoming a published author. Her positive mindset allowed her to persist and eventually achieve success as a best-selling author.

J.K. Rowling has spoken openly about her struggles with depression and how her positive thinking helped her to overcome it. She has said that she would often visualize herself as a successful author and use affirmations to remind her that she had the ability to achieve her dreams. She also made a conscious effort to surround herself with positive and supportive people, including her editor and agent.

Thanks to her positive mindset, J.K. Rowling was able to persist through the many rejections and setbacks she faced on her path to becoming a published author. Her determination, resilience and winning mindset helped her to achieve her goal and become one of the most successful authors of all time.

This story highlights the power of winning mindset, and how it can help individuals overcome obstacles and achieve their goals. J.K. Rowling's positive mindset allowed her to persist through difficult times and ultimately reach her full potential. It's a clear example of the benefits of cultivating a positive mindset and the impact it can have on one's life.

Another example of winning mindset is the story of my father **Sh.G.L.Kumawat.**Growing up in a small village in India, my father knew the meaning of hard work and determination. Despite coming from a poor family, he never let that hold him back from achieving his dreams.

After years of teaching small tuitions and doing stitching work, my father decided to take a risk and move to the city in search of better opportunities. In 1972, he landed a job as a teacher at a school but quickly realized that he wanted something more. He wanted to start his own school and create a better education system for the children in his community.

With just 13 students, my father opened the doors of his own school. He faced countless challenges and obstacles along the way. He had to work hard to gain the trust of parents and the community, face financial struggles, and overcome bureaucratic red tape. But through it all, he remained determined to succeed.

As time passed, his school began to grow. Today, after more than 50 years, that small school has become a network of four branches, educating over 1800 students. My father's vision of a better education system for his community has become a reality.

My father's story is a testament to the power of a winning mindset. He never let fear or doubt hold him back from achieving his dreams. Instead, he used his determination, hard work, and positive thinking to overcome obstacles and create a better future for himself and his community. His story is an inspiration to us all, a reminder that anything is possible with the right mindset and attitude.

An entrepreneur starting a new business, with a winning mindset, this person will be able to think creatively, take calculated risks and persist through the challenges that come with building a successful business. They will also be able to cultivate the resilience to overcome setbacks and stay motivated to continue working towards their goals.

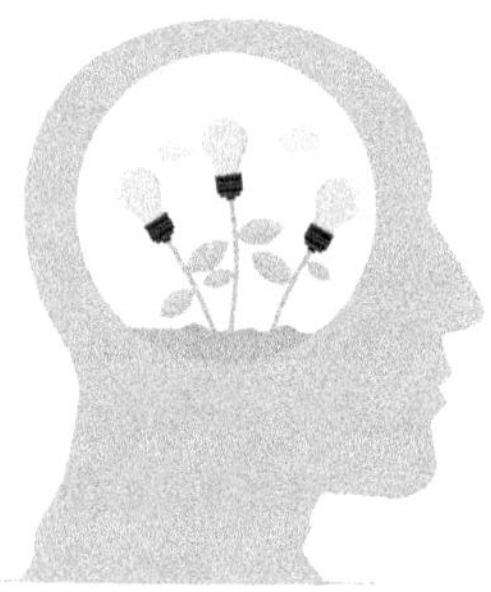

Whether you're an athlete, an entrepreneur, a student, or anyone else, the strategies and techniques outlined in this book will help you develop a winning mindset and achieve success in all areas of your life.

It's important to note that a winning mindset is not something that you are born with; it's something that can be developed and nurtured over time through consistent effort and practice. Everyone has the potential to develop a winning mindset, and this book will provide you with the tools and strategies to do just that.

A student who is struggling with a particular subject, but with a winning mindset, this student will approach the subject with a positive attitude, set clear goals, and persist through the challenges of studying and practicing. He will also develop the resilience to bounce back from setbacks, such as poor test scores, and stay motivated to continue improving.

As you can see, the winning mindset is not just about achieving success in one particular area of life, it's about having the ability to approach any situation with a positive and proactive attitude, and the resilience to overcome any obstacle that comes your way.

Winning is a state of mind. A winning mindset is fundamental to success! Even if you are in the right place and everything goes right, losing will always occur if you don't have a winning mindset.

You've got to have a winning mindset if you want to go far. Just like investing in companies, the right mindset will contribute to your success more than any particular skills or talent.

In the past year I've learned that a successful mindset is essential to winning in business. I've read countless articles about how to be successful and all the information you can find on this subject, but none of those helped me in reaching my goal. Only after I discovered the book 'The Secret' did I understand why. The secret says that we attract what we are. That's why most people who want to succeed never do; they're not attracting success into their life. Their mindset is wrong and they don't realize it, thus they never achieve happiness or success.

The Importance of a Winning Mindset is what I call the ability to control your thoughts. All successful athletes and contestants must have a winning mindset in order to be successful.

It is easy and fun to win when you understand the mindset required. This book provides an overview of the toolkit offered by psychology, which can be applied in any area of life.

Whatever your role in life, there are two elements that are crucial to giving a good account of yourself: resources and mindset. Resources include things like training, education and money, but you also need the right attitude if you want to get the best out of these things or indeed anything else. It's hard work to change your mind if your current outlook is negative and limiting. But you can do it.

The goal of this book is to empower you to develop a winning mindset and achieve success in all areas of your life.

In this book, we will explore the various components of a winning mindset and provide practical strategies for developing and nurturing it.

By reading this book, you will learn how to develop a winning mindset and apply it to your own life. You will learn how to think positively, set and achieve your goals, overcome obstacles, and stay motivated through the ups and downs of life. With the tools and strategies outlined in this book, you will be able to develop a winning mindset and achieve success in all areas of your life.

II

Understanding the Power of Positive Thinking

One of the most important components of a winning mindset is the ability to think positively. Positive thinking is the practice of focusing on the good in any situation and approaching life with a sense of optimism and hope. It is about seeing the glass as half full instead of half empty.

> ""*Positive thinking is not about ignoring the challenges, but about finding the opportunities within them.*""

Positive thinking is the practice of focusing on positive thoughts, emotions, and attitudes in order to improve one's mental and emotional well-being. It is the act of looking for the good in every situation, and choosing to see the world in a positive light. Positive thinking is a mindset that allows an individual to look for the best in people, situations and themselves.

The power of positive thinking cannot be overstated. It has been shown to have a wide range of benefits, including improved mental and physical health, increased resilience, and better overall well-being. It also plays a key role in achieving success and reaching one's full potential.

Positive thinking can also help to improve physical and mental health. Research has shown that positive thinking can help to reduce stress, improve mood, increase self-esteem, and lead to better decision making. Additionally, people who have a positive mindset tend to have better relationships, better job performance and are more likely to achieve their goals.

Positive thinking starts with changing the way we talk to ourselves. This means being mindful of the thoughts that we have and actively choosing to focus on the positive. This can be done through techniques such as positive affirmations, visualization, and gratitude.

Take the example of an individual who is facing a difficult situation, such as a job loss. With a positive mindset, this person will focus on the opportunities that the job loss presents, such as the chance to explore new career paths or take some time to relax and recharge.

They will also use positive affirmations to remind themselves of their strengths and abilities, and use visualization to imagine finding a new job that they love.

An athlete who is facing a losing streak, with a positive mindset, this athlete will focus on the lessons that can be learned from the losses, such as areas for improvement and strategies for success. They will also use positive affirmations to remind themselves of their abilities, and use visualization to imagine winning future games.

Tessa Scott had always been a runner, but she struggled with injuries and self-doubt. She was unable to qualify for the Olympic trials, which was her lifelong goal. However, she refused to let her setbacks define her. She developed a positive attitude, and she decided to focus on her training and her mental game.

She began visualizing herself succeeding, and she developed a strong belief in herself. She worked hard and made sacrifices, and she persevered through injuries and setbacks. She finally qualified for the Olympic trials and went on to represent her country at the Olympics.

Positive thinking also means being mindful of the language we use when talking to ourselves and others. Instead of using negative words and phrases such as "I can't" or "I'll never", we should use positive words and phrases such as "I can" and "I will". This simple change in language can have a powerful impact on our mindset and attitude.

An individual who wants to start a new hobby, with a positive mindset, this person will approach the new hobby with a positive attitude, saying "I can do this" instead of "I can't do this", "I will learn" instead of "I'll never be able to do this". This simple change in language can have a powerful impact on one's mindset and attitude towards the new hobby.

Gratitude is also an important aspect of positive thinking. Being grateful for what we have in life and taking the time to appreciate the good things can help to shift our focus away from negative thoughts and towards the positive.

An individual who is feeling overwhelmed with stress, with a positive mindset, this person will practice gratitude by taking the time to appreciate the good things in their life, such as their health, the support of their loved ones, and the opportunities they have. This simple practice can help shift their focus away from stress and towards the positive aspects of their life.

Another important aspect of positive thinking is being mindful of the company we keep, surrounding ourselves with positive and supportive people can help to foster a positive mindset. On the other hand, being around negative and critical people can bring down our own positive thinking.

It's important to note that positive thinking is not about ignoring or dismissing negative thoughts or experiences, it's about acknowledging them and then choosing to focus on the positive aspects. Positive thinking also does not mean being unrealistic or ignoring problems, it's about approaching challenges and difficulties with a positive attitude and finding solutions.

A person who is trying to change their career, having a friend who is supportive and encourages them to pursue their dreams can help them to maintain a positive mindset and take action towards achieving their goals. On the other hand, having a friend who is negative and critical can make them doubt their abilities and discourage them from pursuing their dreams.

It's also crucial to understand that positive thinking is not just a one-time thing; it's a daily practice that requires effort and consistency. It's something that can be cultivated and developed over time with practice.

An individual who is dealing with a chronic illness, with a positive mindset, this person will approach their condition with a sense of hope and optimism, focusing on the things they can do and the progress they have made. They will also practice gratitude for the support they have and the things they can still do. Positive thinking can help them to cope with the condition and improve their overall well-being.

Research has also shown that positive thinking can have a direct impact on our physical health as well. Positive thinking can help to boost the immune system, lower blood pressure, and reduce the risk of heart disease. It can also help to improve sleep and increase energy levels.

An individual who wants to improve their fitness, with a positive mindset, this person will approach their fitness journey with a positive attitude, setting clear goals, and persist through the challenges that come with sticking to a new exercise routine.

They will also make a daily effort to practice positive thinking by visualizing themselves reaching their goals, using positive affirmations, and focusing on the progress they have made.

It's also important to understand that positive thinking is not just about being happy or having a good mood, it's about having a balanced and healthy outlook on life. Positive thinking can also help to improve our emotional well-being, by reducing stress, anxiety and depression.

An individual who is recovering from a surgery, with a positive mindset, this person will approach their recovery with a sense of hope and optimism, focusing on the progress he has made and the things he will be able to do once he has recovered. He will also practice gratitude for the medical care he has received and for his own strength and resilience. Positive thinking can help to speed up the recovery process and improve his overall well-being.

It's also important to understand that positive thinking is not just for individuals, it's also crucial for organizations and businesses. Positive thinking can help to improve employee engagement, productivity, and creativity in the workplace.

A company that is facing difficult economic times, with a positive mindset, the leadership of the company will approach the situation with a sense of hope and optimism, focusing on the opportunities that the difficult times present and developing strategies to overcome the challenges. They will also practice gratitude for the loyal customers and dedicated employees. Positive thinking can help to improve the overall performance of the company and increase the chances of success.

An individual who is striving to achieve a promotion at work, with a positive mindset, this person will approach the process with a sense of hope and optimism, focusing on the skills he has and the progress he has made. He will also practice gratitude for the support he has received and the opportunities he has been given. Positive thinking can help him to stay motivated and increase his chances of success.

It's also important to remember that positive thinking is not always easy and it's normal to have negative thoughts and feelings. What's important is to acknowledge them, and then make a conscious effort to shift your focus towards the positive.

One way to do this is by keeping a journal and writing down your thoughts and feelings, this can help to identify patterns of negative thinking and allow you to address them. Another way is by practicing mindfulness and being present in the moment, this can help to reduce stress and anxiety and increase positive thinking.

Positive thinking can help to improve our mental and physical health, emotional well-being and overall well-being, and it's not just for individuals, but also for organizations and businesses. Positive thinking can help to improve employee engagement, productivity, and creativity in the workplace. It's a daily practice that requires effort and consistency.

In conclusion, positive thinking is an essential component of a winning mindset. It is about focusing on the good in any situation and approaching life with a sense of optimism and hope. It can be developed and nurtured through techniques such as positive affirmations, visualization, gratitude, and mindfulness of language. By understanding and implementing the power of positive thinking, you will be well on your way to achieving success and reaching your full potential.

III

Setting and Achieving Goals

A winning mindset is not just about overcoming fear and doubt; it's also about setting and achieving goals. Goals give us direction and purpose, and they help to keep us motivated and focused. But let's be real, setting goals is easy, achieving them is the hard part. That's why in this chapter we're going to talk about how to set and achieve goals that will lead to a winning mindset.

Here are the key steps to set and achieve goals:

Start with a vision

A vision is a clear and compelling picture of the future you want to create. It's the starting point for setting and achieving goals. Without a vision, your goals will lack direction and purpose. So, take some time to think about the future you want to create and what that looks like.

Creating a vision is not just about thinking about what you want to achieve, it's about thinking about who you want to become. A vision should be inspiring and motivating, something that you are excited to work towards.

To start creating your vision, ask yourself the following questions:

What is important to me?

What do I want to achieve?

What kind of person do I want to be?

How do I want to feel?

What are my values?

By answering these questions, you can begin to form a clear and compelling picture of the future you want to create. Once you have a vision, you can then start setting specific and measurable goals that align with that vision.

It's also important to remember that your vision can change over time, and that's okay. Life is constantly changing, and your goals and aspirations may change as well. It's important to be flexible and adapt your vision as needed.

Additionally, make your vision visible by creating a vision board or writing your vision statement and putting it somewhere you can see it every day. This will help you to stay focused and motivated as you work towards achieving your goals.

In summary, starting with a vision is crucial for setting and achieving goals. A vision provides direction and purpose, and it helps to keep you motivated and focused. By creating a clear and compelling picture of the future you want to create, you can set specific and measurable goals that align with that vision and work towards achieving them with a winning mindset.

Make your goals SMART

SMART goals are Specific, Measurable, Achievable, Relevant, and Time-bound. This means that your goals should be clear and specific, with a measurable outcome, achievable, relevant to your vision, and have a deadline.

A good example of a SMART goal is "I will save $10,000 in the next 12 months for a down payment on a house."

This goal is specific (saving $10,000), measurable (the specific amount saved), achievable (the goal is realistic and not too ambitious), relevant (the goal is relevant to the individual's vision of buying a house), and time-bound (the goal has a deadline of 12 months).

A story that illustrates the importance of SMART goals is the story of Jane. Jane had always wanted to start her own business, but she didn't know where to start. She decided to set a goal to start her own business within a year. However, she didn't put much thought into it and didn't make it

SMART. A year went by and she still had not started her business.

Frustrated, she decided to start again and this time, she made her goal SMART. She set a specific goal to start her own business selling homemade crafts within 6 months, with a specific target of $5,000 in monthly revenue within the first year. She broke down the goal into smaller actionable steps, such as researching the market, creating a business plan and taking a course on entrepreneurship.

With a clear, specific, measurable, achievable, relevant and time-bound goal, Jane was able to start her own business within six months and reached her revenue target within the first year.

This story illustrates how making a goal SMART can help to increase the chances of achieving it. It gives a clear direction and a deadline, making it more likely to happen. By breaking the goal into smaller actionable steps, it becomes less daunting, and by creating a specific target, it becomes something that is measurable and achievable.

In summary, making your goals SMART is an effective way to ensure that they are specific, measurable, achievable, relevant, and time-bound. By using the SMART method, you can increase your chances of achieving your goals, and a clear and specific goal is more likely to happen, with a deadline and measurable outcome.

Break your goals down into smaller steps

Achieving big goals can feel overwhelming. To make it more manageable, break your goals down into smaller steps. By taking small actions towards your goal, you'll be surprised how quickly you can make progress.

Breaking your goals down into smaller steps is an effective way to make them more manageable and increase the chances of achieving them. It's a process of breaking a large goal into smaller, more manageable tasks that can be accomplished one step at a time.

Here are the steps to break down your goals into smaller steps:

- *Define your goal:* Start by clearly defining your goal, make sure it is specific, measurable, and time-bound.

- *Break down the goal:* Break down the goal into smaller, more manageable tasks. These tasks should be specific, measurable, and actionable.
- *Prioritize the tasks:* Prioritize the tasks that need to be completed by identifying the most critical and urgent tasks first. This will help you to focus on the most important tasks and avoid feeling overwhelmed.
- *Create a plan of action:* Create a plan of action for completing each task, this will help to keep you on track and ensure that you stay on schedule.
- *Set deadlines:* Set deadlines for completing each task, this will help to ensure that you stay on track and make progress towards achieving your goal.
- *Track progress:* Track your progress regularly, this will help you to identify any challenges or obstacles that may arise and make adjustments as needed.
- *Celebrate progress:* Celebrate progress along the way, this will help to keep you motivated and on track to achieving your goal.

Breaking down your goals in this way will help you to stay focused and motivated, it will also help you to track your progress and make adjustments as needed. By breaking down your goals into smaller steps, you can accomplish one step at a time and increase the chances of achieving your goal.

Use positive Self-Talk

Our thoughts shape our emotions and actions. Positive self-talk can help you to stay motivated and focused on your goals. Replace negative thoughts with positive affirmations such as "I am capable and strong" or "I trust in my abilities."

Using positive self-talk is a powerful tool for achieving your goals and developing a winning mindset. Positive self-talk refers to the practice of talking to yourself in a positive and encouraging way. It helps to change negative thoughts and beliefs into positive ones and it can improve your self-esteem, motivation, and overall well-being.

Here are some examples of how to use positive self-talk in detail:

- *Identify negative thoughts*: Start by becoming aware of your negative thoughts. Notice when you have negative thoughts and write them down.
- *Reframe the negative thoughts*: Once you have identified a negative thought, reframe it into a positive one. For example, instead of saying "I can't do this," try saying "I can do this and I will figure out a way to make it happen."
- *Use affirmations*: Affirmations are positive statements that you can repeat to yourself to change negative thoughts and beliefs. For example, "I am capable and strong," "I am worthy of love and happiness," "I believe in myself and my abilities."

- *Practice visualization*: Visualization is the practice of creating a mental image of yourself achieving your goal. Close your eyes and imagine yourself successfully achieving your goal. See yourself as if you have already achieved it.
- *Repeat positive self-talk*: Repeat your positive self-talk, affirmations and visualization regularly, this will help to reprogram your mind and replace negative thoughts with positive ones.
- *Be kind to yourself*: Be kind and compassionate to yourself when you make mistakes or encounter setbacks, instead of being critical. Remember that progress takes time and mistakes are part of the process.
- *Take action*: Positive self-talk can help you to change your thoughts and beliefs, but it's important to take action towards achieving your goal as well.

For example, if someone wants to lose weight, instead of saying "I am too fat and will never be able to lose weight" they should reframe this thought into "I am capable of losing weight, and I will take small steps every day to reach my goal." They can use affirmations such as "I am strong and disciplined in my choices," "I trust in my ability to lose weight," and "I am grateful for my healthy body." They can practice visualization by picturing themselves at their desired weight, feeling confident and happy in their body. They can repeat these positive self-talk statements and visualization regularly, be kind to themselves when they have setbacks, and take action towards their goal by making healthy choices and exercising consistently.

Another example, if someone wants to achieve a promotion at work, they can use positive self-talk to overcome self-doubt and build confidence. Instead of saying "I'm not qualified for this job," they can reframe this thought into "I have the skills and experience to excel in this role." They can use affirmations such as "I am capable and competent," "I am confident in my abilities," and "I am worthy of success." They can practice visualization by picturing themselves in the new role, successfully leading projects and impressing their boss. They can repeat these positive self-talk statements and visualization regularly, be kind to themselves when they encounter challenges, and take action towards their goal by working hard, developing new skills and building relationships with colleagues and supervisors.

In summary, positive self-talk is a powerful tool for achieving your goals and developing a winning mindset. By identifying negative thoughts, reframing them into positive ones, using affirmations, practicing visualization and repeating positive self-talk regularly, you can change your thoughts and beliefs, improve your self-esteem, motivation, and overall well-being. Additionally, it's important to be kind to yourself, and take action towards your goal.

Learn from short stories

There are plenty of short stories that can teach us about setting and achieving goals. Learning from short stories can be a powerful way to gain insight and perspective on different situations and experiences. They can provide examples and lessons that are easy to understand and relate to, and they can be used to teach a wide range of topics such as perseverance, planning, honesty, acceptance and self-esteem. Short stories are an effective tool for teaching because they are easy to understand and relate to, and they can help to illustrate important concepts in a way that is memorable and engaging.

Real-life examples

Real-life examples are a powerful way to illustrate concepts and ideas, making them more relatable and easier to understand. They can be used to show how a particular concept or idea applies in the real world and provide a clear understanding of the practical implications. There are many real-life examples of individuals who have set and achieved goals despite obstacles.

One such example is the story of a celebrity who set and achieved his goals is Viswanathan Anand. He is an Indian chess Grandmaster who has won numerous national and international tournaments. Anand was introduced to chess at a young age and quickly developed a passion for the game. He began playing competitively and quickly made a name for him in the chess world.

Anand set a goal early in his career to become the world chess champion. He worked hard to improve his skills and develop new strategies. He competed in several tournaments around the world and gained valuable experience along the way.

In 2000, Anand finally achieved his goal and was crowned the world chess champion. He continued to dominate the game for many years and became one of the greatest chess players of all time. Anand's success was due to his hard work, dedication, and unwavering commitment to achieving his goals.

Anand's story is a great example of how setting and achieving goals can lead to great success. His determination and perseverance are an inspiration to people of all ages and backgrounds.

Real-life examples can provide a clear understanding of the practical implications and make the concepts relatable and easy to understand. They can also help to motivate and inspire by showing that it is possible to achieve the desired outcome.

Use humor to diffuse stress

Using humor to diffuse stress is an effective way to reduce anxiety and improve mood. Setting and achieving goals can be stressful, but humor can be an effective tool in diffusing stress. Use humor to lighten the mood and make the goal-setting process more enjoyable.Humor can serve as a powerful coping mechanism, providing a temporary distraction from stressors and helping to shift perspective.

Here are a few examples of how humor can be used to diffuse stress:

- *Watch a comedy:* Watching a comedy film or TV show can provide a temporary distraction from stressors and bring a smile to your face. Laughing has been shown to release endorphins, the body's natural feel-good chemicals, which can help to reduce stress and improve mood.

- *Tell jokes or share funny memes*: Telling jokes or sharing funny memes with friends and family can also help to reduce stress. Even if the jokes or memes are not particularly funny, the act of sharing something lighthearted can help to shift the focus away from stressors and bring a smile to your face.

- *Make fun of yourself:* Lightening the mood by making fun of yourself can be an effective way to diffuse stress. This can be a good way to show that you're not taking yourself or the situation too seriously and can help to put things in perspective.

- *Use humor in problem-solving*: Using humor in problem-solving can help to diffuse stress by providing a different perspective on the situation. When faced with a problem, try to find the humor in it and think about how you can use it to your advantage.
- *Find humor in everyday life:* Incorporating humor into your everyday life can also help to diffuse stress. This could be as simple as finding the humor in a traffic jam or a long line at the grocery store.

Humor can be a powerful tool for diffusing stress and improving mood. It can provide a temporary distraction from stressors and bring a smile to your face. The key is to find humor that works for you, whether it's watching a comedy, telling jokes, or making fun of yourself. It's important to remember that humor should be used in a positive and healthy way, never at the expense of others.

Surround yourself with supportive people

The people you surround yourself with can have a big impact on your mindset. Surround yourself with people who will support and encourage you, and who will hold you accountable for achieving your goals. Surrounding yourself with supportive people is an important aspect of developing a winning mindset.

A supportive environment can help to boost your confidence, provide motivation, and offer a sounding board for ideas. Here are a few examples of how surrounding yourself with supportive people can help to develop a winning mindset.

- A *Supportive partner*: Having a supportive partner can provide emotional and moral support, and help to boost your confidence. They can also help you to stay motivated and focused on achieving your goals.
- *Supportive friends*: Having friends who are supportive and encouraging can also help to boost your confidence. They can provide a sounding board for ideas, offer feedback and advice, and help to keep you motivated.
- *Supportive mentors*: Having a mentor who is supportive and encouraging can provide guidance, advice, and help to shape your mindset. They can offer valuable insights and help you to overcome any obstacles or challenges that you may face.
- *Supportive colleagues*: Having colleagues who are supportive and encouraging can help to create a positive work environment. They can provide feedback and help you to stay motivated and focused on achieving your goals.
- *Supportive online communities*: Joining online communities that are supportive and encouraging can

also help to boost your confidence and provide motivation. They can offer a sounding board for ideas and help to keep you motivated and focused on achieving your goals.

In summary, surrounding yourself with supportive people is an important aspect of developing a winning mindset. A supportive environment can help to boost your confidence, provide motivation, and offer a sounding board for ideas. It's important to surround yourself with people who are supportive and encouraging, whether it's a partner, friends, mentors, colleagues or online communities. They can help you to stay motivated, focused and achieve your goals.

Reward yourself for progress

Rewarding yourself for progress is an important aspect of developing a winning mindset and achieving your goals. It helps to acknowledge and celebrate small successes and provides motivation to continue working towards your goal. Setting small goals, recognizing your progress, treating yourself, sharing your progress and celebrating your successes are all ways to reward yourself for progress. It's important to remember that progress takes time and effort, and rewards can help to keep you motivated and focused on achieving your goals.

Keep things in perspective

Setting and achieving goals can be challenging, but it's essential to keep things in perspective. Remember that setbacks and failures are part of the process, and progress takes time. It helps to avoid getting caught up in small setbacks and to focus on the bigger picture.

Here are a few examples of how keeping things in perspective can help to develop a winning mindset:

- *Prioritize*: Prioritizing your goals and focusing on the most important ones can help to keep things in perspective. By focusing on the most important goals, you can avoid getting bogged down by less important tasks and stay focused on what's truly important.
- *Look at the big picture*: When faced with a setback or challenge, take a step back and look at the bigger picture. This can help to put things in perspective and remind you that setbacks and challenges are temporary, and they don't define you or your abilities.
- *Practice gratitude*: Practicing gratitude can help to keep things in perspective by reminding you of what you have to be thankful for. This can help to shift your focus away from negative thoughts and towards positive ones.
- *Learn from failure*: Failure is an inevitable part of the journey towards achieving your goals. Instead of dwelling on failure, learn from it and use it as an opportunity to grow and improve.
- *Seek perspective from others*: Sometimes, it can be helpful to seek perspective from others. Talking to a friend, family member or mentor can help to provide a different perspective and help you to see things in a new light.

In summary, keeping things in perspective is an important aspect of developing a winning mindset. It helps to avoid getting caught up in small setbacks and to focus on the bigger picture.

Prioritizing your goals, looking at the big picture, practicing gratitude, learning from failure and seeking perspective from others are all ways to keep things in perspective. Remember, setbacks and challenges are temporary and don't define you or your abilities, but it's important to keep the big picture in mind, and to focus on what's truly important.

IV

Cultivating Resilience and Mental Toughness

Cultivating resilience and mental toughness is an essential aspect of developing a winning mindset.

Resilience refers to the ability to bounce back from adversity, to adapt and recover from difficult situations, and to maintain a positive outlook despite facing challenges. It is the ability to withstand stress, adapt to change, and recover from setbacks.

Mental toughness, on the other hand, refers to the ability to maintain focus, composure, and determination in the face of adversity or pressure. It is the ability to remain motivated, persistent, and optimistic in the face of challenges and to push through difficult situations. It also includes being able to control one's thoughts, emotions and reactions in order to achieve a goal.

Both resilience and mental toughness are important traits to have in order to achieve success in life, as they help individuals to handle stress, overcome obstacles, and reach their goals. They are a key component of a winning mindset and are essential for achieving personal and professional success.

Here are a few key strategies for cultivating resilience and mental toughness:

Embrace challenges

Embrace challenges as opportunities for growth and development. Instead of avoiding difficult situations, actively seek them out and view them as opportunities to learn and improve. One of the key benefits of embracing challenges is that it allows us to develop grit, which is a combination of passion and perseverance. When we take on challenging tasks, we are forced to push ourselves out of our comfort zone and to work hard to achieve our goals.

Another benefit of embracing challenges is that it helps to develop mental toughness. When we are faced with difficult situations, we are forced to learn how to handle pressure and stress in a positive way. This helps to build the ability to stay focused and motivated in the face of adversity, which is essential for achieving success.

Practice mindfulness

Mindfulness is the practice of being present in the moment and non-judgmental of your thoughts and feelings. One of the key benefits of practicing mindfulness is that it can help to reduce stress and anxiety, which can negatively impact resilience and mental toughness. Mindfulness can help to reduce the negative impact of stress by providing a sense of calm and clarity, which can help to reduce the negative impact of stress and anxiety.

Mindfulness can also help to improve focus and concentration, which are essential for resilience and mental toughness. When we are able to focus our mind, we are able to stay motivated and on task, even in the face of adversity. This helps to build the mental toughness we need to achieve our goals.

Another benefit of mindfulness is that it can help to improve emotional regulation, which is essential for resilience and mental toughness. When we are able to regulate our emotions, we are better equipped to handle stress and to make better decisions.

Furthermore, mindfulness can also help in developing a more positive attitude, which is essential for resilience and mental toughness. By becoming more aware of our thoughts and emotions, we can learn to identify and challenge negative thoughts and beliefs, and replace them with more positive and constructive ones. This can help to build a more positive outlook, which is essential for achieving success.

By incorporating mindfulness into daily life, individuals can develop the ability to handle adversity and stress in a more effective way, and ultimately achieve their goals.

Develop a growth mindset

Having a growth mindset means that you believe that your abilities can be developed through effort and learning. It helps to overcome the setbacks, challenges and obstacles that come your way.

A growth mindset can also help to promote mental toughness, by shifting the focus from being afraid of failure to embracing it as a learning opportunity. When we understand that failure is part of the learning process, we are more likely to take risks and embrace challenges. This can help to build mental toughness and increase our capacity to handle pressure and stress in a positive way.

Get enough sleep

Getting enough sleep is crucial for maintaining a healthy mind and body. Aim for 7-8 hours of sleep each night and try to establish a consistent sleep schedule.

One of the key benefits of getting enough sleep is that it helps to improve cognitive function, including memory, attention, and decision-making. When we are well-rested, our minds are sharper, and we are better able to focus and make better decisions. This is essential for resilience and mental toughness, as it allows us to handle adversity and stress in a more effective way.

Sleep also helps to improve mood, which can impact resilience and mental toughness. Lack of sleep can lead to feelings of irritability, anxiety, and depression, which can negatively impact our ability to handle adversity and stress. Getting enough sleep can help to improve mood and boost energy levels, which can help to improve resilience and mental toughness.

Sleep also plays a critical role in physical health and recovery, which can impact resilience and mental toughness. Adequate sleep is essential for repairing and rejuvenating the body, which can help to improve physical performance and reduce the risk of injury.

Exercise Regularly

Physical fitness and exercise also play an important role in developing resilience and mental toughness. Regular exercise has been shown to improve mood, boost energy levels, and reduce stress. It also helps to build physical and mental toughness. It's important to find an exercise routine that is enjoyable and sustainable, and to make it a regular part of daily life.

Eat a healthy diet

Eating a healthy diet can help to improve energy levels, reduce stress and improve overall well-being. One of the key benefits of eating a healthy diet is that it can help to improve energy levels and overall physical health. A well-balanced diet that includes a variety of fruits, vegetables, whole grains, lean proteins, and healthy fats can provide the necessary energy to handle daily challenges, and to maintain focus and motivation. A balanced diet can also help to reduce the risk of chronic diseases and improve physical performance, which can be beneficial for mental toughness.

Eating a healthy diet can also support brain health and cognitive function, which can be beneficial for resilience and mental toughness. A diet that is rich in fruits, vegetables, and omega-3 fatty acids can help to protect the brain from damage and to promote cognitive function.

Seek help if needed

If you're struggling with resilience or mental toughness, don't be afraid to seek help. Talking to a therapist or counselor can help to provide a different perspective and offer strategies for coping with challenges. Sometimes, despite our best efforts, we may find ourselves struggling to cope with adversity or stress. In such cases, it's important to remember that seeking help is a sign of strength, not weakness. There are various ways to seek help, such as talking to a therapist or counselor, who can help to provide a different perspective and offer strategies for coping with challenges. These professionals can help to identify any underlying issues that may be contributing to the struggle and provide guidance on how to address them. They can also help to provide strategies for managing stress and promoting emotional regulation, which can be beneficial for resilience and mental toughness.

It's also important to consider seeking help from friends and family. Talking to a trusted friend or family member can be a great way to relieve stress, gain new insights, and receive support. They can also help to provide a different perspective and offer practical solutions to problems.

By seeking help when needed, individuals can be better equipped to handle adversity and stress, and ultimately achieve their goals.

In conclusion, the chapter "Cultivating Resilience and Mental Toughness" provides an in-depth examination of the importance of developing a strong and resilient mindset for achieving success. It provides practical strategies and tips for developing grit, mental toughness, emotional intelligence, and a positive attitude. It also encourages you to embrace failure, take calculated risks, and make physical fitness a priority.

It is important to note that developing resilience and mental toughness is a lifelong journey, and that progress will be made through small steps and consistent effort. It is also important to understand that everyone's journey will be different, and it's important to find the strategies and concepts that work best for each individual.

V
Building Self-Confidence

Self-confidence is a crucial ingredient for success in all areas of life. It is the belief in one's abilities, qualities, and judgment. Without self-confidence, it can be challenging to take risks, set and achieve goals, and handle adversity.

"Self-confidence is the first requisite to great undertakings." - Samuel Johnson

In this chapter, we will explore the importance of self-confidence and how it impacts performance, relationships, and overall well-being. We will also delve into the different aspects of self-confidence, including self-esteem, self-worth, and self-assurance. By understanding these concepts, we can develop strategies to build and maintain self-confidence.

One of the most effective ways to build self-confidence is by setting and achieving small goals. Setting small, achievable goals can help to build self-esteem and self-worth. It's important to remember to celebrate small wins and acknowledge progress. Accomplishing small goals can help to build momentum and increase self-confidence.

Another effective strategy for building self-confidence is practicing self-compassion. Self-compassion involves treating oneself with kindness, understanding, and forgiveness. It can be easy to be overly critical of oneself and to compare oneself to others. Practicing self-compassion can help to reduce self-criticism and negative self-talk, which can be detrimental to self-confidence.

Another important aspect of building self-confidence is learning to accept and learn from failure. Failure is a part of life and it's important to understand that it's not a personal failure but rather an opportunity to learn and grow. When we learn to accept and learn from failure, we develop resilience and a growth mindset. This can help to build self-confidence by shifting the focus from fearing failure to embracing it as a learning opportunity.

Physical appearance can also play a role in building self-confidence. Taking care of oneself, such as exercising, eating a healthy diet, and grooming, can improve physical appearance and boost self-confidence. It's important to remember that self-confidence is not just about physical appearance but taking care of oneself can help to improve overall well-being and self-esteem.

Confidence can also be built by developing new skills and knowledge. When we learn new things, we become more capable and capable people are often more confident. It's important to find areas that interest us, and to develop new skills and knowledge in those areas. This will not only help to build self-confidence but also help to improve overall well-being.

In addition, it's important to take care of one's mental health and seek help if needed. Neglecting mental health can lead to negative thoughts, depression, and anxiety which can adversely affect self-confidence. Seeking professional help can be beneficial if one is facing a mental health issue, a therapist or counselor can help to provide a different perspective, and offer strategies for coping with challenges.

Another important aspect of building self-confidence is learning to challenge and overcome limiting beliefs. Limiting beliefs are negative thoughts and self-talk those holds us back and prevent us from achieving our full potential. Examples of limiting beliefs include "I'm not good enough", "I can't do this", and "I'll never be successful". To build self-confidence, it's important to identify and challenge these limiting beliefs by questioning their validity and replacing them with more positive and empowering thoughts.

Another strategy for building self-confidence is to practice assertiveness. Assertiveness is the ability to express oneself in a clear and direct way, without being aggressive or passive. It's important to learn how to set boundaries and communicate needs and wants effectively, this can help to build self-confidence by reducing the fear of rejection or not being heard.

Another important aspect of building self-confidence is learning to manage stress and anxiety. Stress and anxiety can have a negative impact on self-confidence, by causing feelings of insecurity, self-doubt and fear. To build self-confidence, it's important to learn effective stress management techniques such as meditation, yoga, deep breathing exercises, and journaling. These techniques can help to reduce stress and anxiety, and improve overall well-being and self-confidence.

Another strategy for building self-confidence is to focus on personal values and strengths. Personal values and strengths are the things that are most important to us, and that we are naturally good at. By focusing on personal values and strengths, we can build self-confidence by setting goals and working towards achieving them in areas that we are passionate about.

It's also important to practice gratitude and focus on the positive aspects of life. Gratitude is the practice of being thankful for what we have, rather than focusing on what we lack. It's important to take time to reflect on the positive aspects of our lives, and to appreciate them. This can help to improve self-esteem and self-worth, and boost self-confidence.

Another strategy for building self-confidence is to surround oneself with positive role models. Role models are individuals who inspire us and who we look up to. They can be people we know or people we admire from afar. By surrounding ourselves with positive role models, we can learn from their experiences and gain inspiration to build our own self-confidence.

Another way to build self-confidence is through self-expression. Expressing oneself through creative outlets such as writing, art, or music can be a powerful way to build self-confidence. It allows individuals to express their thoughts, feelings, and ideas in a safe and constructive way.

Additionally, it's important to practice self-compassion and self-forgiveness. Self-compassion is the ability to be kind and understanding to oneself, while self-forgiveness is the ability to let go of past mistakes and negative thoughts. These practices can help to reduce self-criticism and negative self-talk, which can be detrimental to self-confidence.

One example of self-confidence playing a vital role in achieving a winning mindset is the story of Serena Williams, one of the greatest tennis players of all time.

Serena was born in 1981 in Michigan, USA, and began playing tennis at a very young age under the guidance of her father, who coached her and her sister Venus. Despite facing racism and sexism throughout her career, Serena refused to let others define her or her abilities. Instead, she relied on her own self-confidence and determination to become one of the most successful athletes in the world.

Early in her career, Serena struggled with self-doubt and suffered several setbacks, including injuries and losses on the court. However, she refused to give up and instead used these experiences as motivation to work harder and improve her game. With each challenge she faced, Serena dug deep and found the inner strength to keep pushing herself forward.

Her hard work and determination paid off, and Serena went on to win a total of 23 Grand Slam singles titles, four Olympic gold medals, and countless other championships and awards. Her incredible success on the court is a testament to the power of self-confidence and the belief that with hard work and determination, anything is possible.

Serena's story shows that self-confidence is not something that comes naturally to everyone. It takes practice, hard work, and a willingness to believe in oneself, even when faced with challenges and setbacks. But with dedication and perseverance, anyone can develop the self-confidence needed to achieve a winning mindset and reach their goals

It's important to remember that building self-confidence is not about being perfect, it's about progress. It's important to be kind to oneself, to celebrate small wins, and to acknowledge progress. Remember that setbacks and failures are a normal part of life and that it's important to learn from them and keep moving forward.

It's also important to recognize that building self-confidence is a personal journey that may require different strategies for different individuals. What works for one person may not work for another. It's important to experiment with different strategies, and to find what works best for you.

In conclusion, building self-confidence is a vital aspect of "The Winning Mindset" and it requires time, effort, and commitment. By understanding the importance of self-confidence and the different aspects of self-confidence, you can develop strategies to build and maintain self-confidence.

VI

The Importance of Visualization and Affirmations

Visualization and affirmations are important tools in the process of achieving goals because they help individuals to focus their thoughts and energy on what they want to achieve.

Visualization allows individuals to create a clear and positive mental image of their desired outcome. This helps to focus their thoughts and energy on what they want to achieve, and to create a roadmap for achieving it. By regularly visualizing their goals, individuals are able to keep their desired outcome in mind and take the necessary steps to achieve it.

Affirmations, on the other hand, are positive statements that individuals repeat to themselves. They are used to reinforce positive thoughts and beliefs about oneself and one's abilities. Affirmations can be powerful in helping individuals overcome limiting beliefs and self-doubt that can hold them back from achieving their goals. By regularly affirming positive statements about oneself, individuals can shift their mindset to one that is more positive and empowering.

Together, visualization and affirmations help to align an individual's thoughts, beliefs, and actions with their desired outcome. This can increase their motivation and drive to achieve their goals, as well as their confidence in their ability to do so. Additionally, visualization and affirmations can help to reduce stress and anxiety that can come with the process of achieving goals, and improve overall well-being.

There are several different aspects of visualization and affirmations, including:

1. **Specificity:** It's important to be specific when visualizing and creating affirmations. The more detailed and specific the visualization or affirmation, the more effective it will be in helping individuals to achieve their goals.

2. **Repetition:** Repeating visualization and affirmations regularly is important for them to be effective. It helps to embed the desired outcome or positive statement into the subconscious mind.

3. **Emotion:** Adding emotion to visualization and affirmations can make them more powerful. For example, visualizing oneself achieving a goal with feelings of excitement and joy can make the visualization more powerful.

4. **Timing:** Finding the right time to visualize and repeat affirmations can also be important. Some people prefer to do it in the morning, others in the evening.

Experiment to find what works best for you.

5. **Environment:** The environment in which visualization and affirmations are practiced can also be important. Finding a quiet and comfortable place can help to reduce distractions and improve focus.

6. **Adaptability**: It's important to be adaptable and flexible with visualization and affirmations. As goals change and evolve, visualization and affirmations should be adapted to align with the new goals.

7. **Combination**:Combining visualization and affirmations can be more powerful than using one or the other alone. Visualizing oneself achieving a goal while repeating affirmations about one's ability to achieve that goal can be a powerful combination.

By understanding these different aspects of visualization and affirmations, individuals can develop strategies to make them more effective in helping them to achieve their goals and improve their self-confidence.

There are several practical tips and techniques that individuals can use to incorporate visualization and affirmations into their daily lives:

1. **Create a visualization board**: Creating a visualization board is a great way to make visualization more tangible and concrete. It involves creating a physical board or collage of images, quotes, and other items that represent one's goals and desired outcome.

2. **Set aside dedicated time for visualization and affirmations:** Setting aside dedicated time for visualization and affirmations can be important for making them a consistent part of one's daily routine. This can be done in the morning or evening, or at any

other time that works best for the individual.

3. **Use guided visualization exercises**: Guided visualization exercises can be helpful for individuals who find it difficult to visualize on their own. These exercises involve listening to a recording that leads the listener through visualization.

4. **Practice in a comfortable and quiet environment**: It's important to find a comfortable and quiet environment to practice visualization and affirmations. This can help to reduce distractions and improve focus.

5. **Incorporate affirmations into daily activities**: Incorporating affirmations into daily activities can help to make them a consistent part of one's routine. For example, repeating affirmations while brushing teeth, cooking, or driving.

6. **Write down your affirmations**: Writing down affirmations can make them more concrete and easier to remember.

7. **Track your progress**: Keeping track of one's progress can help to stay motivated and see the progress that's been made.

By incorporating these practical tips and techniques into their daily lives, individuals can make visualization and affirmations a consistent and effective part of their personal development and goal-achieving journey.

Dr. Kiran Bedi, the first woman IPS officer of India, is a well-known example of someone who used affirmation and visualization to achieve her goals. When she joined the Indian Police Service in 1972, she faced a lot of discrimination and prejudice because of her gender. Many of her colleagues and superiors believed that a woman could not handle the tough and demanding job of a police officer.

However, Dr. Bedi was determined to prove them wrong. She started using affirmations to build her self-confidence and visualize herself as a successful police officer.

She also used visualization techniques to picture herself in various challenging situations that she might face in her job. For example, she would visualize herself defusing a tense situation with a crowd or catching a criminal on the run. By doing this, she was able to prepare herself mentally and emotionally for any situation that might arise.

Dr. Bedi's affirmation and visualization practices paid off in a big way. She quickly rose through the ranks and became the first woman to lead a police force in India. She also initiated several reforms in the prisons and introduced community policing to improve the relationship between the police and the public.

Dr. Bedi's story is a testament to the power of affirmation and visualization in developing a winning mindset. By using these techniques, she was able to overcome the obstacles and challenges that came her way and achieve her goals.

There are several exercises and activities that you can try out in practice visualization and affirmations, including:

1. *Guided visualization exercises:* These exercises involve listening to a recording that leads the listener through visualization. These exercises can be found online or in personal development books.
2. *Journaling prompts:* Journaling can be a great way to reflect on one's visualization and affirmations. Some prompts that can be used include: "What did I visualize today?", "What affirmations did I use today?", and "How

did I feel after visualizing and using affirmations?".

3. *Mind mapping*: Mind mapping can be used as a tool for visualization by creating a diagram that shows the steps needed to achieve a goal.

4. *Storytelling*: Creating a story about the desired outcome, can be a great way to make visualization more concrete and tangible.

5. *Affirmation Jar*: Create an affirmation jar, where you write your affirmations on small pieces of paper, put them in a jar and pick one every day to repeat to yourself.

These are just a few examples of exercises and activities that you can try out and practice visualization and affirmations. By incorporating these exercises and activities into their daily routine, you can make visualization and affirmations a consistent and effective part of your personal development and goal-achieving journey.

In summary, visualization and affirmations play an important role in the process of achieving goals by helping individuals to focus your thoughts and energy on what you want to achieve, overcome limiting beliefs and self-doubt, and align their thoughts, beliefs, and actions with your desired outcome, thus increasing motivation and drive to achieve your goals and building your self-confidence.

VII
Overcoming Adversity and Failure

Adversityrefers to a difficult or challenging situation or circumstance that one must face. It can take many forms, such as financial hardship, illness, relationship problems, or natural disasters. Adversity can also be external, such as a difficult boss or a difficult economic environment, or internal, such as a mental or emotional struggle.

Failure, on the other hand, refers to the state or condition of not achieving a desired outcome. It is often associated with falling short of expectations, whether they are one's own or those of others. Failure can be a result of a lack of skill, knowledge, or resources, or it can be due to unforeseen circumstances. Failure can also be seen as a learning opportunity, as it can provide valuable feedback that can be used to improve future performance.

"The greatest glory in living lies not in never falling, but in rising every time we fall."

- Nelson Mandela

Both adversity and failure can be significant obstacles on the path to success, but they can also be opportunities for growth and development. Those who are able to overcome adversity and failure are often better equipped to handle future challenges and are more likely to achieve your goals

There are many different types of adversity and failure that individuals and organizations may face. Some examples include:

- *Financial adversity*: Difficulty making ends meet, unexpected expenses, or economic downturns.
- *Physical adversity*: Illness, injury, or disability.
- *Relationship adversity*: Difficulty in personal or professional relationships, such as conflict with family members, friends, or coworkers.
- *Natural adversity*: Natural disasters, such as hurricanes, earthquakes, or floods.
- *Professional adversity*: Difficulty in achieving professional goals, such as being passed over for a promotion or losing a job.
- *Mental or emotional adversity*: Struggles with mental health, such as depression or anxiety, or difficulties dealing with stress or emotional challenges.

Similarly, different types of failure can be classified as:

- *Professional failure*: such as loss in business, not getting a desired job, or not succeeding in achieving the expected outcome from a project.
- *Personal failure*: such as not reaching a personal goal, such as losing weight or learning a new language.
- *Academic failure*: such as not passing a test or not getting the desired grades.
- *Social failure*: such as not being accepted by the group or not being able to maintain a friendship.
- *Failure in relationships*: such as not being able to maintain a healthy relationship, or not being able to build one.

It's important to note that these are just examples, and there are many other types of adversity and failure that individuals and organizations may face.

Stephen Hawking, a renowned physicist and cosmologist, was diagnosed with motor neuron disease (also known as ALS or Lou Gehrig's disease) at the age of 21. Despite being given only a few years to live, he went on to become one of the most respected scientists in the world and lived for over 50 years with the disease.

Nelson Mandela, a South African anti-apartheid revolutionary and politician, spent many years in prison for his political activities. After his release, he became the country's first black president and played a crucial role in the dismantling of the apartheid system.

Maya Angelou, an American author and poet, faced a number of difficult experiences in her life, including poverty, racism, and sexual abuse. Despite these challenges, she became a renowned writer and speaker, and her work continues to inspire people around the world.

Vince Lombardi, a coach in American football, turned a losing team into a winning team, and his leadership and coaching methods are still considered a standard in the industry. He faced many failures, including losing seasons and losing in the championship games, but he was able to overcome those by learning from them and using them to improve his team's performance.

Dr. A.P.J. Abdul Kalam, former President of India was born into a humble family and grew up in poverty. Despite this, he was able to excel academically, eventually becoming a renowned aerospace engineer and scientist. He played a key role in India's civilian space program and military missile development.

Dr. Kalam faced many obstacles throughout his career, including limited resources and bureaucratic obstacles, but he never let these setbacks discourage him. He continued to work tirelessly and was able to make significant contributions to the field of science and technology in India.

Later on, Dr. Kalam went on to become the President of India, where he was known as "People's President" and "Missile Man of India" for his work on the development of India's missile programs. He is considered one of the most popular and respected leaders in Indian history and continues to be a source of inspiration for many Indians.

These are just a few examples of individuals who have overcome adversity and failure in your lives. They all show that with determination, perseverance, and the right mindset, it is possible to overcome even the most difficult challenges and achieve great things.

Adversity and failure are an inevitable part of life, but with the right mindset and approach, we can learn to navigate and overcome them.

Practical tips and techniques to overcome from adversity and failure for incorporating strategies into daily life include:

- **Reflecting on past experiences**: Reflecting on past experiences of adversity and failure can be a valuable tool for identifying patterns and developing strategies for addressing similar situations in the future. This can include analyzing what worked and what didn't in past situations, and thinking about the emotions and thoughts that were present. Reflecting on past experiences can also help individuals gain insight into your own strengths and weaknesses, and identify areas for improvement. Reflecting on past experiences can be done through journaling, talking to a therapist or counselor, or simply taking time to think and process past events. It's important to reflect on past experiences in a constructive and non-judgmental way, and to focus on learning from past experiences rather than dwelling on them.

- **Set daily and weekly goals**: Setting daily and weekly goals can help to keep individuals focused and motivated on overcoming adversity and failure. This can include setting specific, measurable, and achievable goals related to building resilience, practicing visualization and affirmations, and working on a plan of action for addressing and overcoming adversity and failure. Setting daily and weekly goals can also include setting aside time for reflection and self-care, and incorporating physical activity into daily routines. When setting daily and weekly goals, it's important to be realistic and to break down larger goals into smaller, more manageable steps. This can make it easier to track progress and stay motivated. Additionally, it's important to regularly review and adjust goals as needed and to celebrate small wins along the way.

- **Create a support network**: Creating a support network of family, friends, and professionals can be an important strategy for overcoming adversity and failure. A support network can provide emotional and practical support during difficult times, and can help to build a sense of community and connection. To create a support network, individuals can reach out to family and friends, join a support group, or seek out a therapist or counselor. It's important to have a variety of people in the support network, from those who can offer practical advice to those who can provide emotional support. It's also important to remember that creating and maintaining a support network takes time and effort, but it can make a big difference in navigating adversity and failure.

- **Find a role model**: Finding a role model who has successfully overcome adversity and failure can be a valuable strategy for gaining inspiration and guidance on how to navigate difficult situations. A role model can be someone who is well-known, such as a public figure or historical figure, or someone in one's personal life. For example, if an individual wants to overcome financial adversity, they can look up to someone like Oprah Winfrey, who grew up in poverty and built a media empire. Or if an individual wants to overcome a physical adversity, they can look up to someone like Wilma Rudolph, who overcame polio as a child and went on to become a world-renowned Olympic runner. These real-life examples show that it's possible to overcome adversity and achieve success, regardless of the odds. By studying your experiences, strategies, and mindset, it can give an idea on how to approach similar challenges in the future.

- **Keep a journal:** Keeping a journal can be a helpful tool for reflecting on thoughts, feelings, and experiences related to adversity and failure. Journaling allows individuals to process their emotions and gain insight into their own thoughts and patterns. For example, if an individual is going through a difficult period of their life, they can use journaling to reflect on their emotions, thoughts and the actions they took during that time.

This can help them identify patterns and develop strategies for addressing similar situations in the future. Another example is an individual who is trying to overcome a fear or phobia, they can use journaling to document their progress, thoughts, and feelings during the process. It can also be used as a tool for tracking progress, setting and achieving goals, and monitoring mental and emotional well-being. Writing down thoughts and feelings in a journal can also provide a sense of release and can be a form of self-care.

- **Recognize and challenge limiting beliefs**: Recognizing and challenging limiting beliefs can be an important step in overcoming adversity and failure. Limiting beliefs are negative thoughts and assumptions that hold individuals back from achieving their goals. For example, an individual who believes they are not smart enough to succeed in a certain field, may not even try to pursue it, limiting their potential. Another example is an individual who believe that they are not worthy of love or affection, might push people away and avoid forming healthy relationships.

Recognizing and challenging limiting beliefs can be done by becoming aware of them, questioning them and replacing them with more positive and empowering thoughts. Examples of empowering thoughts are "I am capable and worthy of success" or "I am deserving of love and affection". This process can be aided by seeking professional help, such as a therapist or counselor. It's important to remember that changing limiting beliefs takes time, effort and practice, but it can help individuals to achieve their goals and improve their self-confidence.

By incorporating these practical tips and techniques into daily life, individuals can make strategies for overcoming adversity and failure a consistent and effective part of their personal development and goal-achieving journey.

Amitabh Bachchan, one of the most iconic actors in Indian cinema, has faced several failures and adversities in his career. However, he has always bounced back with a positive attitude and a determination to overcome the tough times.

One of the most significant setbacks that Amitabh Bachchan faced was in 1982 when he suffered a near-fatal accident on the set of the movie "Coolie." He had to undergo multiple surgeries and was in critical condition for several weeks. During this time, the entire nation prayed for his recovery, and his fans were devastated by the news of his accident.

However, Amitabh Bachchan did not let this setback defeat him. He emerged stronger and more determined than ever. Despite the physical and emotional trauma he had experienced, he continued to work hard and strive for excellence in his career.

In the early 2000s, Amitabh Bachchan's career was not in a good direction. He had gone through a string of unsuccessful films, and his popularity had dwindled. It was during this time that he was approached to host the Indian version of the popular game show "Who Wants to Be a Millionaire?" - "Kaun Banega Crorepati" (KBC).

Initially, Amitabh Bachchan was hesitant to take up the offer. He had never hosted a television show before, and he was not sure if he could connect with the audience. However, his wife Jaya Bachchan convinced him to take up the challenge, and he agreed to host the show.

KBC turned out to be a massive success, with viewers tuning in to watch Amitabh Bachchan's charismatic and engaging hosting style. The show's format, which involved asking contestants a series of increasingly difficult questions to win a cash prize, also resonated with audiences. KBC became one of the most-watched television shows in India, and Amitabh Bachchan became a household name once again.

The success of KBC not only revived Amitabh Bachchan's career but also transformed his public image. He was no longer seen as just a movie star but as a charismatic and knowledgeable personality who could connect with people across different age groups and backgrounds.

Through his resilience and determination, Amitabh Bachchan has become an inspiration to millions of people in India and around the world. His success story shows that with hard work, perseverance, and a positive attitude, one can overcome even the toughest challenges and emerge victorious.

It is important to remember that setbacks and failures are a natural part of the journey to success, and that the most successful individuals and organizations are those who are able to learn from their mistakes and keep moving forward.

VIII

The Power of Persistence and Determination

When we think about success, we often think about talent and intelligence. But the truth is, some of the most successful people in the world are not the most talented or intelligent. They are the ones who are the most persistent and determined.

Persistence is the ability to continue working towards a goal despite obstacles or difficulties. It is the quality of continuing to do something even when it is hard or not immediately successful. It is the ability to keep going, to keep pushing forward, and to not give up in the face of adversity.

Determination is the quality of being firmly resolved to do something. It is the willpower and drive to achieve a goal despite any obstacles or challenges that may arise. Determination is the inner conviction that you can and will succeed, no matter what. It is the steadfastness in purpose and the unwavering commitment to achieving success.

In short, persistence is the act of continuing to do something, while determination is the mindset or attitude that drives that persistence. Persistence is the action and determination is the mindset that drives the action.

One of the most famous examples of persistence and determination is the story of Milkha Singh, also known as the Flying Sikh, who was one of India's most successful track and field athletes.

Singh was born in a small village in Punjab in 1935 and had a difficult childhood. He lost his parents during the partition of India and Pakistan in 1947 and had to flee to India with his siblings. Despite these challenges, Singh discovered a talent for running and began training in the sport.

In the late 1950s and early 1960s, Singh represented India in numerous international competitions, including the Olympics. However, he faced stiff competition from some of the world's best runners and initially struggled to win medals.

In the 1960 Rome Olympics, Singh narrowly missed out on a medal in the 400 meters race, finishing fourth. This defeat spurred him on, and he began training even harder. He went on to set multiple national records and win numerous medals in international competitions.

Singh's most famous victory came in the 1962 Asian Games, where he won gold medals in the 400 meters and 4x400 meters relay events. He also set a new Asian Games record in the 400 meters, which stood for over 40 years.

Singh's success on the track made him a national hero in India, and his story of perseverance and determination continues to inspire people to this day.

Ratan Tata, one of India's most successful businessmen, is also a great example of persistence and determination. He faced many challenges throughout his career, but he never gave up. He worked hard, took calculated risks and never lost sight of his goal. His persistence and determination paid off, and he went on to build one of India's most successful companies.

But you don't have to be a famous inventor or author to benefit from persistence and determination. These qualities can help you in every area of your life, from school to sports to your career.

For example, if you're having trouble with a difficult math problem, you can use persistence to keep working on it until you find the solution. If you're trying to make a sports team, you can use determination to keep practicing and working hard, even when you don't make the cut. And if you're trying to start a business, you can use persistence to keep pushing through the tough times and determination to make it a success.

Sachin Tendulkar, one of the greatest cricketers of all time, is a prime example of persistence and determination. He faced many challenges throughout his career, but he never gave up. He worked hard, practiced tirelessly, and never lost sight of his goal. His persistence and determination paid off, and he went on to become one of the greatest cricketers in the world.

It's important to note that persistence and determination don't mean blindly continuing on a path that is clearly not working. It's important to be adaptable and willing to change your approach if something isn't working. But it does mean not giving up and always looking for ways to improve and move forward.

Development of Persistence and Determination

Developing persistence and determination is not something that happens overnight, it is a habit that needs to be developed over time.

- It's important to have a clear vision of what you want to achieve, this will give you a clear reason to persist and be determined. When you know what you're working towards, it's easier to stay motivated and keep going, even when things get hard.
- Another important aspect is to Regularly review and reflect on your progress, and make adjustments to your plan if necessary.
- Mindfulness can help you to stay focused and present in the moment, which can be beneficial when working towards a goal. Meditation can help you to reduce stress

and increase focus, which can help to improve your ability to persist and be determined.

- Creating a sense of accountability can help to increase persistence and determination. This can involve sharing your goals with friends and family, or even a coach or mentor. Having someone to be accountable to can provide motivation and support, and can help to increase your commitment to achieving your goals.

Finally, it's important to take care of yourself and manage your stress levels. Persistence and determination are admirable qualities, but they can also lead to burnout if you don't take the time to take care of yourself. Make sure to set aside time for rest and relaxation, and practice stress-management techniques such as meditation or yoga.

Dhirubhai Ambani , who was an Indian business tycoon and entrepreneur who founded Reliance Industries, one of India's largest conglomerates. He came from a small village in Gujarat and started out as a small-time trader. Despite facing numerous obstacles and challenges in his journey, including lack of formal education, lack of financial resources, and lack of industry connections, he never gave up. He was determined to succeed and was persistent in his efforts to build his business. He worked hard and never gave up in the face of adversity. He was able to turn Reliance Industries into one of India's most successful and influential companies, and his story is often cited as an inspiration for entrepreneurs and business leaders in India and around the world.

Persistence and determination work together to help individuals and organizations achieve success. Persistence is the ability to continue working towards a goal despite obstacles or difficulties, while determination is the willpower and drive to achieve that goal. Together, they provide the necessary mindset and actions to overcome any challenges that may arise on the path to success.

For example, an individual with determination will set a goal for themselves and make a plan to achieve it, but without persistence, they may give up at the first sign of difficulty. On the other hand, an individual with persistence may continue working towards a goal, but without determination, they may lack the drive and motivation to see it through to completion. Together, persistence and determination provide the necessary mindset and actions to overcome any challenges that may arise on the path to success.

Additionally, determination can help to fuel the fire of persistence, by providing the motivation to keep going and not giving up, while persistence can help to keep determination grounded, by providing the willingness to stick with a plan, even when it gets difficult. Together they make a powerful combination, they can help individuals and organizations to overcome obstacles, adapt to changing circumstances, and achieve success.

In conclusion, the power of persistence and determination is the key to success in any area of life. When you're faced with a challenge, remember the stories of Milkha Singh , Ratan Tata , Sachin Tendulkar, and Dhirubhai Ambani keep pushing forward. With persistence and determination, you can achieve anything you set your mind to.

IX

Self - Discipline and Self – Control

Self-discipline and self-control are essential qualities that are closely connected to the concept of a winning mindset. A winning mindset is characterized by a strong focus on goals, a positive attitude, and a willingness to persevere through challenges and obstacles. Self-discipline and Self-control are critical components of this mindset as they allow individuals to stay focused on their goals, resist distractions and temptations, and make the necessary sacrifices to achieve success.

Both are essential qualities that required achieving success in any area of life. They are the foundation of a strong, resilient and productive mindset. Self-discipline is the ability to control one's actions, emotions, and thoughts in order to reach a goal. It is the ability to resist instant gratification and to delay gratification for a greater goal. On the other hand, self-control is the ability to control one's impulses, emotions, and actions in order to make better decisions. Together, self-discipline and self-control are powerful tools that can help individuals to achieve their goals and overcome obstacles.

Self-discipline and self-control are critical in developing a sense of responsibility and ownership of one's actions. By being self-disciplined and having self-control, individuals are able to take responsibility for their decisions and actions, and are less likely to make excuses for their failures. This mindset shift is key in developing a sense of personal accountability and ownership that is necessary for achieving long-term success.

People with self-discipline and self-control are better able to resist negative thoughts and emotions, and to maintain a positive outlook even in the face of challenges. They are also more likely to adopt a growth mindset and to see challenges as opportunities for growth and learning.

Moreover, self-discipline and self-control are essential for making the best choices and decisions, whether in personal or professional life, which is crucial for a winning mindset. It allows individuals to have a clear understanding of what they want, and to make deliberate choices that align with those goals. This leads to more consistent and effective action, and ultimately, to greater success. They allows individuals to think things through, weigh the pros and cons, and make deliberate, well-thought-out decisions that align with their goals and values.

There are many examples of individuals who have achieved success through self-discipline and self-control. One well-known example is Warren Buffett, the legendary investor and businessman. He is widely considered to be one of the most successful investors of all time, and his success is attributed in part to his remarkable self-discipline and self-control.

Buffett is known for his ability to stay focused on his long-term goals and to resist the temptations and distractions that can derail progress. He is also known for his ability to make deliberate, well-thought-out decisions and to stick to his investment principles, even in the face of market volatility and uncertainty. Additionally, he has a strong work ethic, he spends most of his day reading and analyzing financial reports, which has been key to his success.

Kalpana Chawla, the first Indian-American astronaut, who demonstrated self-discipline and self-control to achieve her goal of becoming an astronaut. She went through rigorous training, which was challenging and required a lot of self-discipline and self-control. She was able to persist through the challenges and obstacles and ultimately achieve her goal.

Additionally, self-discipline and self-control are also important in developing resilience, which is an integral part of a winning mindset. People who are self-disciplined and have self-control, tend to be more adaptable and better equipped to handle adversity. They are more likely to learn from their failures and to bounce back from setbacks. This can help them to be more resilient in the face of challenges and obstacles, which is crucial for achieving long-term success.

Athletes like Michael Phelps, Michael Jordan and Players like Roger Federer ,MS Dhoni are also great examples of individuals who have achieved success through self-discipline and self-control. These athletes & players are known for their rigorous training regimes, their ability to stay focused on their goals, and their ability to perform at the highest level under pressure.

Furthermore, having self-discipline and self-control also enhances the ability to learn and grow, which is vital for a winning mindset. One example of an individual who has used self-discipline and self-control to enhance their ability to learn and grow is Virat Kohli.Kohli is an exemplary example of self-discipline and self-control for achieving a winning mindset. His dedication to training and focus on improving his game has been the cornerstones of his career. Kohli is a great believer in the power of hard work and practice and has consistently sought to challenge himself in order to stay ahead of the competition. He is known to have rigorous training sessions, studying his opponents and analyzing their strengths and weaknesses. He also has a strict diet and fitness plan, which he has to adhere to in order to maintain his peak performance.

Additionally, Kohli is a very patient and humble person. He never looks to take shortcuts and is always willing to learn from his mistakes and make necessary changes. His mental strength and resilience in the face of tough challenges has served as an example of how to remain focused and motivated. Finally, Kohli also demonstrates a never-say-die attitude that helps him stay motivated and driven in tough times. His persistence and dedication have enabled him to become one of the most successful cricket players in the world.

Benefits of Self-discipline and Self-control

The benefits of self-discipline and self-control are numerous and can have a profound impact on an individual's personal and professional life. Some of the key benefits include:

- *Increased productivity and efficiency*: Self-discipline and self-control allow individuals to focus on what is important, prioritize tasks, and manage time effectively, leading to increased productivity and efficiency.
- *Improved decision making*: Self-discipline and self-control allow individuals to think more clearly and make better decisions. This is because they are less likely to be swayed by emotions and impulses, and more likely to consider all options and choose the best course of action.
- *Greater success in achieving goals*: Self-discipline and self-control are essential for achieving goals. They allow individuals to set clear and specific goals, make progress towards achieving them, and stay on track even when faced with obstacles.
- *Better relationships*: Self-discipline and self-control can also improve relationships. This is because individuals who are self-disciplined and self-controlled are more reliable, dependable, and trustworthy, and are better able to manage their emotions and impulses.
- *Enhanced mental and physical well-being*: Self-discipline and self-control can also lead to enhanced mental and physical well-being. This is because individuals who are self-disciplined and self-controlled are more likely to engage in healthy habits, such as regular exercise and healthy eating, and less likely to engage in unhealthy habits, such as smoking and excessive alcohol consumption.

- *Increased confidence and self-esteem:* Self-discipline and self-control can also lead to increased confidence and self-esteem. This is because individuals who are self-disciplined and self-controlled are more likely to achieve their goals, and this can lead to a sense of accomplishment and pride.
- *Greater resilience and adaptability:* Self-discipline and self-control also help individuals to be more resilient and adaptable. They can handle stress and adversity better and can quickly rebound from failure.

Overall, self-discipline and self-control are essential for achieving success in all areas of life. They allow individuals to set and achieve their goals, manage their time and emotions effectively, and make better decisions.

Development of Self-discipline and Self-control

Developing self-discipline and self-control is a process that requires time, effort, and commitment. We can develop it with the help of following points.

1. **Prioritizing tasks and managing time effectively:** Self-discipline and self-control are closely linked to time management. Prioritizing tasks and managing time effectively allows individuals to focus on what is important and avoid wasting time on less important tasks. This also allows individuals to make progress towards their goals in a timely manner.

2. **Building healthy habits and routines:** Developing self-discipline and self-control requires building healthy habits and routines. This includes things like regular exercise, healthy eating, and adequate sleep. These habits and routines help individuals to maintain focus, stay motivated, and prevent burnout.

3. **Staying accountable and tracking progress:** Self-discipline and self-control require accountability and tracking progress. This means regularly evaluating progress towards goals, noting successes and failures, and making adjustments as necessary. This helps individuals to stay on track, stay motivated, and make progress towards their goals.

4. **Overcoming procrastination and distractions:** Self-discipline and self-control require overcoming procrastination and distractions. This means identifying and eliminating sources of procrastination and distractions, setting clear and specific goals, and staying accountable and tracking progress.

5. **Managing emotions and impulses:** Self-discipline and self-control also require managing emotions and impulses. This means learning to recognize and manage emotions and impulses that can lead to procrastination, distractions, and failure. This includes things like anger, fear, and anxiety.

By following these strategies, individuals can develop self-discipline and self-control, and make progress towards achieving their goals. This will ultimately lead to success in their personal and professional life.

People who are self-disciplined and have self-control tend to be more open to new ideas, more willing to take risks, and more likely to seek out new opportunities for growth. This can lead to greater personal and professional development, which is essential for achieving long-term success

In a winning mindset, self-discipline and self-control also help in managing and regulating emotions, which is essential for staying focused and maintaining a clear mind.

With self-discipline and self-control, individuals are better able to handle stress, anxiety, and other negative emotions that can impede progress.

Furthermore, self-discipline and self-control are also important in developing a strong work ethic, which is a vital trait of a winning mindset. Oprah's work ethic is well-known, her dedication to her craft and her commitment to producing high-quality content has been a major factor in her success. People who are self-disciplined and have self-control , tend to be more productive, efficient, and consistent in their work. They are able to prioritize their tasks and to make the most of their time, which leads to greater output and productivity.

X

The Role of Mindfulness and Self-Awareness in the Winning Mindset

The concept of mindfulness and self-awareness has been gaining popularity in recent years, especially in the field of personal development and achievement. In this chapter, we will explore the connection between mindfulness, self-awareness, and the winning mindset. We will also provide steps that you can take to apply these practices in your own life.

Mindfulness and self-awareness are closely connected to the winning mindset, as they both involve gaining a deeper understanding of yourself and your motivations.

This understanding can lead to greater self-control, improved decision-making, and ultimately, greater success in achieving your goals.

Mindfulness is the practice of being present and fully engaged in the current moment, without judgment. It involves paying attention to your thoughts, feelings, and physical sensations in a non-judgmental way. Self-awareness, on the other hand, is the ability to understand and acknowledge your own thoughts, emotions, and behaviors.

Together, mindfulness and self-awareness can help you to gain a deeper understanding of yourself and your motivations by allowing you to observe and acknowledge your thoughts, emotions, and behaviors in a non-judgmental way. By being present in the moment and paying attention to your internal experience, you can gain insight into patterns and habits that may be holding you back or pushing you towards your goals.

For example, mindfulness can help you to become aware of negative thought patterns or self-talk that may be preventing you from achieving your goals. With this awareness, you can then make a conscious choice to challenge and change these thoughts, which can lead to greater self-control and improved decision-making. Additionally, self-awareness can help you to identify your core values and what truly matters to you, which can guide you in setting and achieving meaningful goals.

Furthermore, Mindfulness and self-awareness can help you to become more aware of your own emotions and how they affect you. For example, if you are feeling anxious, you may be more likely to make impulsive decisions or react negatively to certain situations. With mindfulness and self-awareness, you can learn how to recognize these emotions as they arise, and then take steps to manage them in a more effective way, such as by taking deep breaths, or engaging in a mindfulness exercise.

To apply mindfulness and self-awareness in your own life, there are several steps that you can take:

Start a daily meditation practice

Starting a daily meditation practice can be extremely helpful in developing mindfulness and self-awareness. Meditation is a powerful tool that can help to quiet the mind, allowing you to focus on the present moment and observe your thoughts, emotions, and physical sensations without judgment.

When you meditate, you learn to observe your thoughts without getting caught up in them. Instead of getting lost in a stream of thoughts, you learn to simply acknowledge them and let them pass. This can help to reduce feelings of stress and anxiety, and can also help to increase your ability to focus and concentrate.

In addition, meditation can also help to cultivate self-awareness by allowing you to observe your thoughts, emotions, and physical sensations in a non-judgmental way. This can help you to gain insight into patterns and habits that may be holding you back, and can also help you to identify your core values and what truly matters to you.

Furthermore, meditation can help to improve the connection between your mind and body, which can be helpful in developing self-awareness. By focusing on your breath and the sensations in your body, you can learn to become more aware of your physical sensations and how they relate to your thoughts and emotions. This can be useful in developing self-awareness and understanding your own emotions.

Keep a journal

Writing down your thoughts and feelings can help you to gain a deeper understanding of yourself and your motivations. Keeping a journal can be a powerful tool in developing mindfulness and self-awareness. It can help you to process and make sense of your thoughts, emotions, and experiences, and can also help you to identify patterns and habits that may be holding you back.

When you journal, you are able to reflect on your thoughts and emotions in a more structured way, which can help you to gain insight into your own mental and emotional landscape. For example, if you are struggling with a specific problem or decision, writing about it in your journal can help you to explore your thoughts and feelings related to it, and may help you to gain a new perspective.

Additionally, journaling can also help to cultivate self-awareness by allowing you to observe your thoughts and feelings in a non-judgmental way. This can help you to identify patterns and habits that may be holding you back, such as negative self-talk or impulsive decision-making, which can be changed by bringing them to your awareness.

Furthermore, journaling can also help to track your progress over time. For example, you can journal your thoughts and feelings before and after a mindfulness or meditation practice, and observe how you feel differently over time. This can help you to understand the effect of your practices and make adjustments as needed.

Practice mindfulness throughout the day

This can be as simple as taking a moment to focus on your breath and be present in the moment, or even just taking a few minutes to focus on the sensations in your body. Practicing mindfulness throughout the day can be extremely helpful in developing mindfulness and self-awareness. Mindfulness is the practice of being present and fully engaged in the current moment, without judgment. By practicing mindfulness throughout the day, you can learn to be more present and aware of your thoughts, emotions, and physical sensations, which can lead to greater self-awareness and understanding of yourself and your motivations.

Additionally, practicing mindfulness throughout the day can also help you to become more aware of your physical sensations and how they relate to your thoughts and emotions. This can be useful in developing self-awareness and understanding your own emotions. For example, if you notice that you feel tense or anxious, you can take a moment to focus on your breath and release the tension, rather than reacting impulsively.

Furthermore, practicing mindfulness throughout the day can also help to improve your overall well-being and reduce stress. By taking a moment to be present in the moment, you can learn to let go of distracting thoughts and focus on what truly matters, which can lead to a greater sense of peace and contentment.

Reflect on your actions and behavior

Take time to think about the choices you make and the actions you take, and consider how they align with your goals and values. Reflecting on your actions and behavior can be extremely helpful in developing mindfulness and self-awareness. It involves taking time to think about the choices you make and the actions you take, and considering how they align with your goals and values. This can help you to gain a deeper understanding of yourself and your motivations, which can lead to greater self-awareness and self-control.

For example, by reflecting on your actions and behavior, you can become more aware of patterns and habits that may be holding you back, such as procrastination or impulsive decision-making. With this awareness, you can then make a conscious choice to change these patterns and habits, which can lead to greater self-control and improved decision-making.

Additionally, reflecting on your actions and behavior can also help you to identify your core values and what truly matters to you. This can guide you in setting and achieving meaningful goals that align with your values and passions.

By taking time to reflect on your actions and behavior, you can learn to let go of distracting thoughts and focus on what truly matters, which can lead to a greater sense of peace and contentment.

There are several common mistakes that people make when practicing mindfulness and self-awareness:

1. *Expecting immediate results*: Mindfulness and self-awareness are practices that take time and patience to develop. It's important to be patient with yourself and not to get discouraged if you don't see immediate changes.
2. *Trying to change yourself*: Mindfulness and self-awareness are not about trying to change yourself or your thoughts and feelings, but rather about observing

and acknowledging them. Accepting yourself as you are is an important aspect of self-awareness.

3. *Treating it as a one-time thing*: Mindfulness and self-awareness are not a one-time thing, but rather a continuous practice that should be integrated into your daily life. It's important to make time for these practices on a regular basis.

4. *Getting too caught up in technique:* Mindfulness and self-awareness are not about achieving a particular state of mind or perfecting a technique. Instead, it is about being present and aware in the moment, without judgment.

5. *Neglecting self-compassion:* It's easy to be hard on yourself when practicing mindfulness and self-awareness, but it's important to remember to be kind and compassionate with yourself. Treat yourself with the same kindness and understanding that you would offer to a friend.

6. *Not distinguishing between mindfulness and relaxation:* Mindfulness and relaxation are not the same thing, mindfulness is about being aware of your thoughts, emotions and sensations, while relaxation is about letting go of stress and tension. It's important to distinguish between the two and not to confuse them.

In summary, It's important to be patient, consistent and non-judgmental in your practice, not to expect immediate results, not to try to change yourself, to make time for these practices on a regular basis, not to get too caught up in technique, to treat yourself with self-compassion and distinguish between mindfulness and relaxation.

When you practice mindfulness, you learn to be present and fully engaged in the current moment, without judgment. This can help you to focus on the task at hand, rather than getting caught up in distractions or negative thoughts. This focus and clarity of mind can help you to make better decisions, which can lead to greater success.

Self-awareness, on the other hand, is the ability to understand and acknowledge your own thoughts, emotions, and behaviors. By becoming more self-aware, you can gain insight into patterns and habits that may be holding you back, and make conscious choices to change them. This can lead to greater self-control and improved decision-making, which can be crucial in achieving your goals.

Furthermore, by understanding your core values and what truly matters to you, which can be gained through mindfulness and self-awareness practices, you can set and achieve meaningful goals that align with your passions. This can increase motivation and improve the chances of achieving your goals.

In summary, Mindfulness and self-awareness are closely connected to the winning mindset, as they both involve gaining a deeper understanding of yourself and your motivations. This understanding can lead to greater self-control, improved decision-making, and ultimately, greater success in achieving your goals. It also can increase motivation, improve focus and clarity of mind, and guide you in setting and achieving meaningful goals that align with your passions.

XI

Support System and Mentors

The path to success is not an easy one. It requires hard work, dedication, and perseverance. However, it is not only the individual's effort that determines their success but also the support system and mentors that they surround themselves with. In this chapter, we will discuss the importance of support systems and mentors in developing a winning mindset. We will explore the benefits and harms that a support system and mentors can have, as well as things to consider when building and maintaining them. Additionally, we will examine the stories of successful individuals, both past and present, who have relied on their support systems and mentors to achieve their goals.

A support system refers to the network of people who provide emotional, practical, and/or financial support to an individual. This can include family, friends, colleagues, and professional resources such as therapists or coaches.

A mentor is an experienced and trusted advisor who provides guidance, advice, and support to a mentee. A mentor can help the mentee develop new skills, gain new perspectives, and navigate the challenges of their career or personal life. A mentor can be a role model, advisor, and teacher.

The Importance of Support Systems & Mentor

Support systems & Mentor are an essential aspect of a winning mindset. A support system is a group of individuals who provide emotional and practical support to an individual. These individuals can include friends, family, colleagues, and even acquaintances. They play a vital role in an individual's ability to navigate and succeed in their chosen field.

Having a strong support & Mentor system can provide a sense of belonging and connection, which can boost an individual's mental and emotional well-being. A support system can also provide practical assistance, such as helping with childcare or providing financial assistance. Furthermore, a support system can provide a sounding board for ideas, allowing individuals to bounce ideas off of others and gain valuable feedback.

A support system & a Mentor can also be a source of motivation and inspiration. The members of a support system can provide encouragement and support, which can be especially important during times of stress and uncertainty.

Additionally, a Support system & Mentor can provide an outside perspective on situations, which can be valuable in problem-solving and decision-making. A support system can also be a source of accountability, which can help an individual stay on track and achieve their goals.

Benefits of Support Systems & Mentor

Support systems & Mentor can provide a variety of benefits for individuals working towards a winning mindset. Some of these benefits include:

1. **Emotional and mental well-being**: A support system & Mentor can provide a sense of belonging and connection, which can boost an individual's mental and emotional well-being. This can be especially important during times of stress and uncertainty.
2. **Practical assistance**: Support systems & Mentor can provide practical assistance, such as helping with childcare or providing financial assistance. This can help alleviate some of the stress and responsibilities that come with pursuing success.
3. **Sounding board for ideas**: A support system & Mentor can provide a sounding board for ideas, allowing individuals to bounce ideas off of others and gain valuable feedback. This can be especially important for entrepreneurs and individuals in creative fields.
4. **Encouragement and support**: A support system & Mentor can be a source of motivation and inspiration.

The members of a support system can provide encouragement and support, which can be especially important during times of stress and uncertainty.

5. **Outside perspective**: A support system & Mentor can provide an outside perspective on situations, which can be valuable in problem-solving and decision-making. This can be especially useful when an individual is too close to a situation to see it objectively.

6. **Accountability**: A support system & Mentor can serve as a source of accountability, which can help an individual stay on track and achieve their goals. This can be especially important for individuals who have a tendency to procrastinate or lack self-discipline.

Examples:

- A professional athlete may rely on their support system & Mentor to provide emotional and mental support during the highs and lows of their career. They may also rely on their support system & Mentor to help them manage their schedule and finances.
- An entrepreneur may rely on their support system & Mentor to provide feedback on their business ideas and provide practical assistance in starting their business.
- A student may rely on their support system & Mentor to provide encouragement and support during the stress of exams and assignments, and also to provide practical assistance such as studying together or sharing notes.

In conclusion, support systems & Mentor can provide a variety of benefits for individuals working towards a winning mindset, including emotional and mental well-being, practical assistance, a sounding board for ideas, encouragement and support, an outside perspective and accountability.

Harms of Support Systems & Mentor

However, support systems & Mentor can also have negative effects. Individuals may feel pressure to conform to the opinions and beliefs of their support system & Mentor, rather than following their own intuition and values. Additionally, if the support system & Mentor is not a healthy one, it can lead to negative effects on an individual's mental and emotional well-being.

Things to Consider when Building a Support System & Mentor

Building a strong support system & Mentor is essential for achieving success and developing a winning mindset. However, it is important to consider certain factors when building a support system to ensure that it is effective and beneficial. Some things to consider when building a support system include:

1. *Alignment of values and goals*: It is important to surround oneself with individuals who have similar values and goals. This can ensure that the support system & Mentor is composed of individuals who understand and support the individual's aspirations.

2. *Positive and supportive individuals*: It is important to surround oneself with positive and supportive individuals. This can help to boost an individual's mental and emotional well-being and provide a source of encouragement and inspiration.

3. *Balance of practical and emotional support*: It is important to have a balance of individuals who can provide practical assistance, as well as those who can provide emotional support. This can ensure that the support system & Mentor can provide a wide range of support and assistance.

4. *Trust and transparency*: It is important to have trust and transparency within the support system & Mentor. This can ensure that the support system is a safe space for individuals to share their thoughts and feelings without fear of judgment or ridicule.

5. *Regular check-ins*: It is important to have regular check-ins with the members of the support system & Mentor. This can ensure that the support system is meeting the individual's needs and that any issues or concerns can be addressed in a timely manner.

6. *Availability and accessibility*: It is important to have a support system & Mentor that is available and accessible to the individual. This can ensure that the support system & Mentor can provide assistance and support when it is needed.

Examples:

- A business owner might consider building a support system made up of colleagues, mentors, and other business owners in the same industry. This can provide valuable feedback and advice, as well as a sounding board for ideas.
- A student might consider building a support system made up of classmates, professors, and friends. This can provide a source of encouragement and support during the stress of exams and assignments, and also provide practical assistance such as studying together or sharing notes.

In conclusion, building a strong support system is essential for achieving success and developing a winning mindset. It is important to consider factors such as alignment of values and goals, positive and supportive individuals, balance of practical and emotional support, trust and transparency, regular check-ins, and availability and accessibility when building a support system. This can ensure that the support system is effective and beneficial in helping the individual to achieve their goals.

Michael Jordan, one of the greatest basketball players of all time. Michael credits his mentor and former coach, Dean Smith, for teaching him the importance of hard work, perseverance, and humility. Dean Smith not only taught Michael the skills he needed to succeed on the court but also instilled in him the values and mindset necessary to become a true champion.

Chandragupta Maurya was a great Indian emperor who founded the Maurya dynasty. Chanakya was his mentor and advisor, who helped Chandragupta in his conquests and laid the foundation for his success.

Chanakya was a brilliant strategist and scholar who recognized Chandragupta's potential and took him under his wing. He not only taught Chandragupta the art of warfare and statecraft but also imparted valuable life lessons that shaped Chandragupta's character.

Chandragupta faced numerous challenges and obstacles during his reign, but with Chanakya's guidance and support, he overcame them all. Chanakya's wisdom and guidance helped Chandragupta develop a winning mindset that enabled him to overcome his fears and doubts.

One such incident that highlights the importance of a support system and mentor in a winning mindset is the story of Chandragupta's conquest of the kingdom of Magadha. The ruler of Magadha, King Dhanananda, was a powerful and ruthless king who had defeated many of his enemies. Chandragupta knew that defeating Dhanananda would be a difficult task, but he was determined to succeed.

Chanakya advised Chandragupta to build a strong support system by forming alliances with other kings and gaining their support. He also helped Chandragupta develop a winning mindset by teaching him to believe in himself and his abilities.

Chandragupta followed Chanakya's advice and formed alliances with several other kings. Together, they marched towards Magadha and engaged in a fierce battle with Dhanananda's army. Chandragupta's army emerged victorious, and he became the new king of Magadha.

Chandragupta's victory over Dhanananda was not just a result of his military prowess but also due to his strong support system and the guidance of his mentor Chanakya. This incident highlights the importance of having a support system and a mentor who can provide guidance and support during difficult times, especially in developing a winning mindset.

In essence, the support of a strong support system and mentors is essential in developing a winning mindset. Support systems provide emotional and practical support, while mentors provide guidance and advice on how to navigate the challenges of pursuing success. A mentor, an experienced and trusted advisor, can help individuals gain new skills, perspectives, and navigate the challenges of their career or personal life. Both support system and mentorship can act as a guide in difficult times, providing encouragement and advice to individuals on their journey to success. However, it is important to carefully choose both support system members and mentors to ensure they align with your values and goals. Learning from the experiences of successful individuals, such as Michael Jordan,Nelson Mandela and Chandragupta Maurya can provide inspiration and guidance on the path to success.

XII

Staying Motivated and Focused

Motivation and focus are essential elements of a winning mindset. They provide the drive and determination necessary to push through obstacles and achieve success. However, staying motivated and focused can be a challenge, especially in the face of setbacks and disappointments. In this chapter, we will explore the importance of staying motivated and focused, as well as strategies and techniques for doing so.

Defining Motivation

Motivation is the psychological and emotional forces that drive individuals to take action. It is the underlying energy that propels us to pursue our goals and aspirations. Motivation can come from within (intrinsic motivation) or from external sources (extrinsic motivation). Understanding the sources of motivation can help individuals tap into their own internal drive and find ways to sustain it.

Intrinsic motivation comes from personal interest or enjoyment in a task, while extrinsic motivation comes from external rewards or pressures. Intrinsic motivation is generally considered more powerful and sustainable than extrinsic motivation as it is self-driven.

Motivation can change over time and in response to different situations. It can fluctuate depending on factors such as one's mood, level of stress, or external circumstances. Understanding how motivation can change can help individuals develop strategies for maintaining and increasing motivation in different situations.

Defining Focus

Focus is the ability to direct one's attention and concentrate on a specific task or goal. It is the ability to filter out distractions and stay on task, which is essential for achieving goals and reaching success.

There are different types of focus, such as short-term vs. long-term focus. Short-term focus is used for completing specific tasks or goals, while long-term focus is used for working towards larger, long-term goals.

Focus can be improved and strengthened through practice and training. Techniques such as meditation, mindfulness, and goal-setting can help individuals improve their focus and concentration.

The relationship between motivation and focus

Motivation drives one to focus on a task or goal. Without motivation, individuals may lack the energy and drive to stay focused and work towards their goals.

Focus helps to maintain motivation by keeping individuals on track and making progress towards their goals. When individuals are focused, they are more likely to make progress and feel a sense of accomplishment, which can increase motivation.

A lack of motivation or focus can hinder progress and lead to procrastination or stagnation. Without motivation, individuals may lack the drive to start a task or goal, and without focus, they may struggle to stay on task and make progress.

By understanding the relationship between motivation and focus, individuals can develop strategies for maintaining both and achieving success.

One of the most important factors in staying motivated and focused is setting clear and achievable goals. Goals provide a sense of direction and purpose, and give individuals something to strive for. Setting specific, measurable, attainable, relevant, and time-bound (SMART) goals can help to keep individuals motivated and focused.

Another important factor in staying motivated and focused is having a positive attitude. A positive attitude can help to counteract negative thoughts and feelings, and can provide a sense of hope and optimism. This can be especially important during times of stress and uncertainty.

Developing a daily routine can also be an effective way to stay motivated and focused. Having a set routine can provide a sense of structure and order, and can help to keep individuals on track. This can include setting aside time each day for exercise, meditation, or other activities that promote well-being.

Taking regular breaks and practicing self-care can also be important in staying motivated and focused. Allowing oneself to rest and recharge can help to prevent burnout and can provide a renewed sense of energy and focus.

Another important factor in staying motivated and focused is having a clear plan of action. Having a specific plan of action with defined steps and deadlines can help to keep individuals on track and focused. It also helps to break down big goals into smaller, manageable tasks and make the goal seem more achievable.

Another important factor in staying motivated and focused is being able to manage stress and anxiety. Stress and anxiety can be major distractions and can erode motivation and focus. It is important to learn effective stress management techniques such as deep breathing, meditation, or exercise to help cope with stress and anxiety.

Lastly, it is important to be self-aware and to be mindful of one's own thoughts and emotions. Self-awareness can help individuals to identify negative thoughts and emotions that may be hindering motivation and focus. By being mindful of one's own thoughts and emotions, individuals can take steps to change negative patterns and maintain a positive outlook.

In conclusion, there are several factors to consider when trying to stay motivated and focused, including having a sense of purpose, having a clear plan of action, managing stress and anxiety, and being self-aware and mindful of one's own thoughts and emotions. By understanding and addressing these factors, individuals can develop the resilience and determination necessary to achieve success and develop a winning mindset.

One example of staying motivated and focused *Mahendra Singh Dhoni,* also known as MS Dhoni, is a former Indian cricketer and captain of the Indian national team. He is widely regarded as one of the greatest cricketers of all time, and his story is a prime example of staying motivated and focused.

Dhoni grew up in a small town in India and faced numerous challenges on his journey to becoming a professional cricketer. He worked hard to improve his game and eventually made his debut for the Indian team in 2004. Despite facing criticism and setbacks many times in his career, Dhoni remained focused on his goals and never lost his motivation.

One of the key factors that helped Dhoni stay motivated and focused was his calm and composed demeanor, even under pressure. He was known for his ability to stay cool and make rational decisions, even in high-pressure situations. This quality earned him the nickname "Captain Cool" and helped him lead the Indian team to numerous victories, including the 2007 ICC World Twenty20 and the 2011 ICC Cricket World Cup.

Another factor that helped Dhoni stay motivated and focused was his dedication to his fitness and training. He was known for his rigorous training regime and strict diet, which helped him maintain his physical and mental strength.

Overall, MS Dhoni's story is a testament to the power of perseverance, focus, and determination. His ability to stay motivated and focused on his goals, despite facing numerous challenges and setbacks, is an inspiration to millions of people around the world.

In conclusion, MSDhoni's story illustrates how staying motivated and focused can help in the winning mindset. His ability to set specific, measurable goals, develop a growth mindset, have a clear sense of purpose, pay attention to his well-being, and have a positive attitude helped him to overcome obstacles and achieve success in his career.

Another example of staying motivated and focused helping in the winning mindset can be seen in the story of Prime Minister Narendra Modi of India. Despite facing numerous challenges and obstacles throughout his political career, Prime Minister Modi remained focused on his goal of serving the people of India and working towards the development and progress of the country.

He set specific, measurable goals for his government, and worked tirelessly to achieve them through various initiatives and policies. He had a deep sense of purpose and passion for serving his country, which helped him to stay motivated and focused throughout his political career. He also had a strong support system of party members and advisors who provided guidance and inspiration.

Prime Minister Modi has a positive attitude and is known for his resilience and ability to adapt to changing circumstances. He also has a strong work ethic, which helps him to manage stress and stay focused on his goals. He has a growth mindset, and believes that change is possible through hard work and determination, this helped him to overcome obstacles and achieve success in implementing policies and initiatives for the welfare of the nation.

Prime Minister Narendra Modi's story illustrates how staying motivated and focused can help in the winning mindset. His ability to set specific, measurable goals, have a clear sense of purpose and passion, have a strong support system, have a positive attitude, have a growth mindset and manage stress helped him to overcome obstacles and achieve success in his political career and contributions to the development of India.

In conclusion, staying motivated and focused is essential for achieving success and developing a winning mindset. Remember to stay focused and motivated to achieve your goals and you'll find yourself more productive and fulfilled.

ॐ

XIII

Conclusion: Putting the Winning Mindset into Action

Congratulations on reaching the end of this book! We hope that you have found the information and insights provided to be useful in understanding the concept of the winning mindset and how to apply it in your own life.

As we have discussed throughout this book, the winning mindset is a combination of various mental and emotional factors that can lead to greater success in achieving your goals. These include having a positive attitude, setting clear and achievable goals, taking action, being resilient in the face of challenges, and cultivating mindfulness and self-awareness.

Developing a winning mindset begins with understanding the power of positive thinking. By harnessing the power of positive thinking, individuals can improve their mental and physical health, emotional well-being, and overall well-being. This concept is not limited to individuals but also applies to organizations and businesses. Positive thinking can lead to increased productivity, improved relationships, and greater success in achieving goals. It is a crucial step in creating a winning mindset that can lead to long-term success in all areas of life

In achieving the winning mindset fear and doubt can be major obstacles to a winning mindset, but by understanding that these emotions are natural and normal, and taking small steps to overcome them, we can reach our full potential. Surround yourself with positive people, challenge negative thoughts, and find humor in difficult situations

To put the winning mindset into action, it's important to start by setting clear and achievable goals for yourself. These should be specific, measurable, and time-bound, and should align with your values and passions. It's also important to take action towards your goals, and to be persistent and resilient in the face of challenges.

In addition, it's important to cultivate a positive attitude and maintain a growth mindset. This means being open to learning and growth, and viewing challenges as opportunities for growth rather than as obstacles.

Building self-confidence is a vital aspect of "The Winning Mindset" and it requires time, effort, and commitment. Managing stress and anxiety, focusing on personal values and strengths, practicing self-compassion and self-forgiveness, and recognizing that building self-confidence is a continuous process are all effective strategies for building self-confidence.

Finally, cultivating mindfulness and self-awareness can be extremely helpful in developing the winning mindset. By being present in the moment and aware of your thoughts, emotions, and physical sensations, you can gain a deeper understanding of yourself and your motivations, which can lead to greater self-control and improved decision-making.

It's important to remember that the winning mindset is not just about achieving external success, but also about developing inner peace, contentment, and fulfillment. By aligning your goals with your values and passions, and by cultivating mindfulness and self-awareness, you can learn to find joy and satisfaction in the present moment, regardless of whether or not you have reached your external goals.

Additionally, it's also important to remember that the winning mindset is not a destination, but a continuous journey. It takes consistent effort and practice to develop and maintain the winning mindset. It's essential to be patient with yourself and not to get discouraged if you don't see immediate changes.

In conclusion, the winning mindset is a combination of various mental and emotional factors that can lead to greater success in achieving your goals. Remember that success is a journey, and by consistently applying the principles of the winning mindset, you can make progress towards achieving your goals. We encourage you to take the information and insights provided in this book and apply them in your own life, and to continue to strive for personal growth and success.

About The Author

Dr..Rajnish Kumawat is an author of this book.He has demonstrated his commitment to academics by earning a PhD in computer science and has used his knowledge to make contributions to the field. His passion for writing is evident in the books he has published, which showcase his creativity and storytelling skills.

He is not just limited to writing technical content, but he has also written books on various other subjects that showcase his versatility as a writer.

In addition to his writing pursuits, he also has a love for blogging and shares his thoughts and ideas with the world through his personal blog.

He has also written many poems in both Hindi and English. His book, "Family in Poetic Prose," is a beautiful collection of family poem that shows the importance of each member of family.